Mental Illnesses and Disorders

DEPRESSION

**Feeling Worthless • Loss of Interest • Difficulty Sleeping
Low Energy • Difficulty Making Decisions**

H. W. Poole

www.av2books.com

AV² provides enriched content that supplements and complements this book. Weigl's AV² books strive to create inspired learning and engage young minds in a total learning experience.

Your AV² Media Enhanced books come alive with...

Audio
Listen to sections of the book read aloud.

Key Words
Study vocabulary, and complete a matching word activity.

Go to **www.av2books.com,** and enter this book's unique code.

Video
Watch informative video clips.

Quizzes
Test your knowledge.

BOOK CODE

AVF49488

Embedded Weblinks
Gain additional information for research.

Slide Show
View images and captions, and prepare a presentation.

AV² by Weigl brings you media enhanced books that support active learning.

Try This!
Complete activities and hands-on experiments.

... and much, much more!

Published by AV² by Weigl
350 5th Avenue, 59th Floor
New York, NY 10118
Website: www.av2books.com

Library of Congress Control Number: 2018941330

ISBN 978-1-4896-8086-0 (hardcover)
ISBN 978-1-4896-8087-7 (softcover)
ISBN 978-1-4896-8088-4 (multi-user eBook)

Printed in Brainerd, Minnesota, United States
1 2 3 4 5 6 7 8 9 0   22 21 20 19 18

072018
120817

Project Coordinator: Heather Kissock Designer: Ana María Vidal

Every reasonable effort has been made to trace ownership and to obtain permission to reprint copyright material. The publisher would be pleased to have any errors or omissions brought to its attention so that they may be corrected in subsequent printings.

Weigl acknowledges Getty Images, iStock, Shutterstock, and Alamy as its primary image suppliers for this title.

First published by Mason Crest in 2016.

DEC 1 0 2019

Contents

AV² Book Code   2

Chapter 1
What Is Depression?   4

Chapter 2
Other Types of Depression   10

Chapter 3
Getting Help   16

Chapter 4
Managing Depression   22

Depression over Time   28
Quiz   30
Key Words/Index   31
Log on to www.av2books.com   32

What Is Depression?

Think about something you love to do. It could be drawing or soccer. It could be going on a hike, watching a movie, or just hanging out with your best friend. It could be anything. Just picture yourself doing that activity. Think about how good you feel when you do it.

Now picture yourself doing that same activity, but imagine the good feelings are not there. The activity that you normally enjoy no longer makes you happy. Even something great, like scoring a goal or drawing a perfect picture, does not give you the happiness it normally would. Your best friend's jokes are not funny. Your favorite movie now just seems stupid. Imagine that all the good stuff just feels like ... nothing. This is an indication of what it feels like to be depressed.

People suffering from depression may find that even being with friends does not lift their mood. Depressed people may cut themselves off from friends over time.

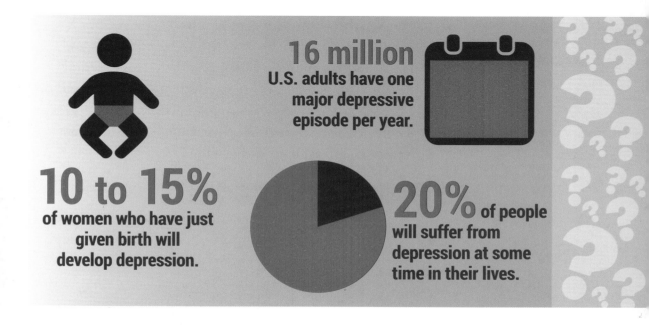

16 million U.S. adults have one major depressive episode per year.

10 to 15% of women who have just given birth will develop depression.

20% of people will suffer from depression at some time in their lives.

More than Sad

The verb to "depress" means "to push something down." People who have depression tend to feel rather "pushed down." They are often tired. They feel empty inside. Things they used to love just do not appeal to them anymore. Having depression is different from being sad.

Everybody feels sad sometimes. It is a normal part of life. If something bad happens, such as a loved one dies, it is normal to feel sad for a long time. However, people who feel sad about an event will start to feel better in time. It might take a while, but people bounce back.

Major depressive disorder is more common in women than in men.

People with depression can bounce back, too, but it can be harder. They may need help from friends and family. Sometimes, they may need help from mental health professionals. People with depression can, and do, get better. There are ways to help people with depression. There are also **strategies** for battling depression that a person can use him- or herself.

Major Depressive Disorder

There are different types of depression that can occur. The two main types are major depressive disorder and persistent depressive disorder. The type of depression called major depressive disorder is probably what most people think of when they talk about depression.

Doctors use a specific set of **criteria** to make a diagnosis. If someone has at least five of the symptoms below for several weeks, he or she is experiencing a major depressive episode (MDE).

- Feeling sad, empty, or hopeless, most of the time on most days

- Loss of interest in activities that used to be enjoyable

- Noticeable weight loss or weight gain, usually a loss or gain of at least 5 percent of body weight

- Difficulty sleeping or sleeping too much

- Low energy on most days

- Feeling worthless or guilty with no obvious reason why

- Difficulty thinking or making decisions

- Low energy on most days

- Regular thoughts of death or suicide

What Is a Mood Disorder?

A mood disorder is a condition rooted in the brain that affects the way a person thinks, feels, and acts. Depression is a type of mood disorder that involves feeling bad most or all of the time. Another type is called bipolar disorder, which involves swings between feeling "too good" and "too bad." The Centers for Disease Control and Prevention (CDC) estimates that almost 1 in 10 people suffers from depression each year. According to the American Academy of Child and Adolescent Psychiatry, 1 in 20 children has some form of depression.

Symptoms of MDE can be **subjective**, meaning they are reported by the person experiencing them. They can also be **objective**, meaning that family, friends, or teachers notice the changes. Often, mental health professionals use a combination of subjective and objective observations. For example, a girl who is having an MDE might admit that she has trouble sleeping but claim that she is not sad. Instead, it might be her mother who notices that she has lost interest in her hobbies, while her doctor might be the one who notices her weight loss.

Persistent Depressive Disorder

This type of depression used to be called dysthymia, an ancient Greek word that means, roughly, "bad frame of mind." The symptoms of persistent depressive disorder are mostly the same as major depressive disorder, but there are a few key differences.

One big difference is the amount of time involved. To be diagnosed with persistent depressive disorder, an adult must have symptoms for two years, or just one year in children. Another difference is the **severity** of the symptoms. A child who is having a major depressive episode might skip school constantly. She might not be able to get out of bed at all. On the other hand, a child with persistent depressive disorder is probably able to get through the school day, just not very happily. It is more of a **chronic** problem. It is not as dramatic, but it drags on and on without getting better.

Depression can change a person's relationship with food. Some depressed people eat a lot more, while others do not feel like eating much at all.

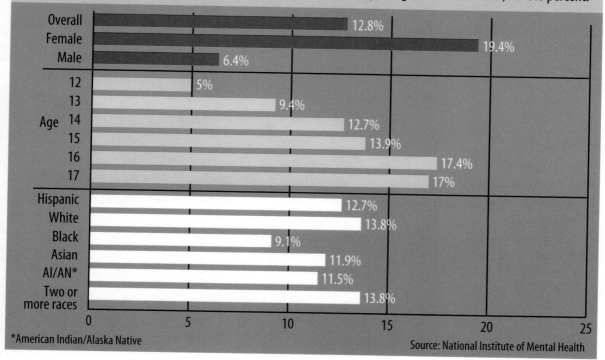

MAJOR DEPRESSIVE EPISODES AMONG U.S. ADOLESCENTS

In 2016, an estimated 3.1 million adolescents, or 12.8 percent of the population aged 12 to 17, had at least one MDE. More adolescent females, at 19.4 percent, compared to males, at 6.4 percent, had an MDE. The incidence of MDE was higher among white adolescents and those reporting two or more races, at 13.8 percent.

Overall: 12.8%
Female: 19.4%
Male: 6.4%

Age
12: 5%
13: 9.4%
14: 12.7%
15: 13.9%
16: 17.4%
17: 17%

Hispanic: 12.7%
White: 13.8%
Black: 9.1%
Asian: 11.9%
AI/AN*: 11.5%
Two or more races: 13.8%

*American Indian/Alaska Native

Source: National Institute of Mental Health

Persistent depressive disorder can start at a young age. This can make the disorder very difficult to spot. People might assume the person is naturally moody or has an unhappy personality. Even the person with the disorder might not realize that there is something wrong, thinking that is just the way he or she feels.

Causes of Depression

Doctors do not know exactly why some people develop depression. Like many mental disorders, there are probably a number of factors. Doctors do know that brain chemistry plays a huge role in people's moods. Depression often results from the brain producing either too much or too little of the chemicals it needs to work properly. Traumatic experiences can also cause depression, as can family problems or unexpressed anger.

Other Types of Depression

Depression is the most common type of mental disorder. The CDC reports that 26 percent of U.S. adults struggle with it every year. Researchers are still trying to figure out what causes the two most common types of depression. However, other types of depression can be caused by specific events that occur either inside or outside the body.

Seasonal Affective Disorder

During the winter, days get shorter because either the northern or the southern hemisphere of Earth is farther away from the Sun. In the northern hemisphere, the middle of winter is in December. In the southern hemisphere, it is in June.

Winter means that the temperature gets colder and there are fewer hours of sunshine. A lack of sunlight can affect people's moods. Sometimes, this results in a form of depression that doctors call major depressive disorder with seasonal pattern. More commonly, this problem is called seasonal affective disorder (SAD).

It is not surprising that people might feel unhappy when the weather is bad and they cannot spend much time outside. However, being a little down is not the same thing as having SAD.

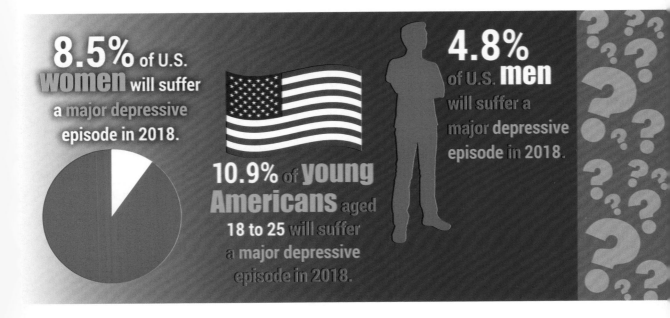

8.5% of U.S. **women** will suffer a major depressive episode in 2018.

10.9% of **young Americans** aged 18 to 25 will suffer a major depressive episode in 2018.

4.8% of U.S. **men** will suffer a major depressive episode in 2018.

Light therapy is safe and has no side effects, and it can ease the symptoms of SAD.

People who have SAD show the same symptoms of depression as people with the other types of depression. They include feelings of sadness or emptiness, loss of interest in favorite activities, low energy, and problems with sleeping or weight.

The difference is, once the seasons change, people with SAD feel better. The season, which is usually winter but not always, is a **trigger** for their depression. On the one hand, that is good news. At least people with SAD know that their feelings will not last forever. On the other hand, there are lots of places where winter weather can last for months. It is too long a time to be that miserable.

Some treatments can be effective for SAD. One treatment is called light therapy. The person sits with a special light that is similar to sunlight. People can also take a natural supplement called melatonin, which is sometimes helpful in easing SAD. Exercise, taking walks outside, and talking to a counselor can also help. If the situation is severe, a doctor might prescribe a medication called an antidepressant to help the person stay positive during the winter months.

Depressive Disorder and Medical Conditions

A person with a headache might also feel a little irritable. That is easy to understand. It is hard to be cheerful when something in the body hurts. Fortunately, when the headache goes away, so will the bad mood. However, the situation is different when people are sick for a long period of time. A person who has an illness such as diabetes or cancer can feel not only unwell but also scared.

People with long-term physical challenges often struggle with depression in addition to their illnesses. There are also particular illnesses that cause depression. Brain injuries, Alzheimer's disease, Parkinson's disease, and multiple sclerosis can all cause depression along with their other symptoms.

A New Type of Depression

When diagnosing patients, mental health professionals use criteria described in the *Diagnostic and Statistical Manual of Mental Disorders* (*DSM*). The most recent version, the *DSM-5*, includes a new category of depression, which applies only to children, called disruptive mood dysregulation disorder (DMDD). Children with DMDD have a chronic bad temper. They get irritated or frustrated very easily. They have angry outbursts multiple times per week. This makes it very hard for them to get along with other people or to do well in school. Previously, these children might have been diagnosed with a disruptive behavior disorder, bipolar disorder, or even autism. Doctors hope that the new category will help prevent children from being misdiagnosed as bipolar or autistic when their problems lie elsewhere.

Problems with an underactive **thyroid** can cause people to be depressed. Many people who struggle with alcohol or drug addictions also suffer from depression, either because they are trying to quit or because they believe that quitting is impossible. Anyone with a chronic physical condition and depression symptoms can get help from the doctor or another trusted adult. No one should have to feel sad and hopeless all the time, just because of an illness.

Disorders Unique to Women

Bringing new life into the world is an amazing ability that only females have. This feat requires hormonal changes as well as a monthly experience called **menstruation**. Unfortunately, these changes in hormone levels can lead to depressive disorders in some girls and women.

Depression can have a severe impact on the health of older adults. Many studies have shown that depression is associated with worse health in people with illnesses such as heart disease or diabetes.

PREMENSTRUAL DYSPHORIC DISORDER. People also call this PMS, which is short for premenstrual syndrome. In the days before a woman menstruates, her hormone levels change. She might have aching joints or muscles, and her body may retain extra water. She may feel physically uncomfortable and emotionally just a little off balance.

Most of the time this is not a huge problem. Pain relievers such as aspirin or ibuprofen can help. The symptoms pass soon after menstruation begins. However, in some women, the symptoms are very severe, and they look and feel a lot like those of depression. Doctors call this premenstrual dysphoric disorder (PMDD). It can lead to monthly problems at school or work, as well as problems in relationships. It is not uncommon for someone with PMDD to have another disorder as well, such as SAD or anxiety.

POSTPARTUM DEPRESSION. Giving birth is an intense experience. Some women experience a lot of problems after having a baby, in what doctors call the **postpartum** period. It is natural for new mothers to feel overwhelmed. They are now responsible for a helpless baby who needs attention 24 hours a day. Meanwhile, their bodies are still recovering from pregnancy and childbirth. New mothers might cry a lot, feel exhausted, and get irritated easily. Usually, these feelings are balanced with the joy of having a new baby. When things are out of balance, when frustration and misery overwhelm all the good feelings, a mother might have postpartum depression.

Many women feel anxious and depressed after having a baby. That usually disappears in about two weeks. However, women with postpartum depression can experience major depression for months.

Postpartum depression can be treated, just like every other type of depression. With therapy and medication, it usually goes away in a few months. If a new mother seems depressed, her feelings should not be overlooked. In a tiny number of cases, a very serious disorder called postpartum **psychosis** can develop. A woman with postpartum psychosis may become so overwhelmed with despair that she hurts herself or her child. This problem can also be treated, but this should be done in a hospital setting.

Chapter 3
Getting Help

Some mental disorders are fairly obvious to observers. If someone has schizophrenia, for example, the symptoms, such as disorganized speech, can be easy to spot. Often, depression is not like that. People all go through periods where they feel down. It can be hard to tell what is a "normal" sad mood and what is a disorder. In particular, the chronic type of depression called persistent depressive disorder can be very hard to spot.

A doctor might have advice for dealing with depression, or he or she might suggest that the patient see a mental health professional.

Getting Help

If you often feel hopeless, tired, and empty inside, or if you know someone who seems that way, it is important to talk to a trusted adult, such as a family member or teacher. You could even start with a friendly neighbor or a responsible older child, such as a sibling or babysitter. If someone experiences depressive symptoms for more than a few weeks, it is time to see a doctor. Treatment for children often starts with a **pediatrician**. Pediatricians mostly focus on the body, but they can also recognize mental disorders.

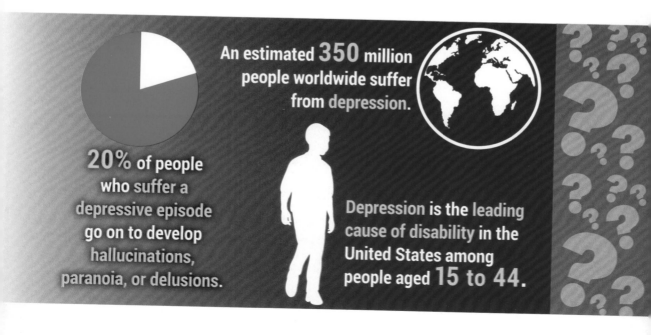

An estimated 350 million people worldwide suffer from depression.

20% of people who suffer a depressive episode go on to develop hallucinations, paranoia, or delusions.

Depression is the leading cause of disability in the United States among people aged 15 to 44.

The initial discussion with a mental health professional may take an hour or more as he or she asks questions to build a full picture of a person's physical and mental health.

First Visit

During a first visit with a mental health professional, he or she will ask a lot of questions. Some of the questions will be about the patient's general health and whether he or she has problems with sleep or appetite. He or she will be asked about feeling tired, hopeless, or suicidal, feeling fidgety and restless, or whether he or she is having difficulty concentrating or making decisions. It may seem overwhelming to answer all these personal questions. However, it is important to be honest, because the answers will help the therapist figure out what is wrong. In many cases, the mental health professional will be able to identify what disorder a patient has just from the facts and observations he or she makes during this first visit. At that point, the mental health professional will discuss with the patient, and a parent or another trusted adult if appropriate, what the treatment should be. It could involve talk therapy or medication, or both.

Taking Medicine for Depression

The brain is like a giant communications center. In order for the body to function, the brain must communicate with every other part of the body. Billions of messages are sent and received throughout the brain in a single day. To do this, the brain uses a complex network of nerve cells called neurons. Neurons do not touch each other. There are spaces between each neuron, which are called synapses.

Disorders Due to a Medical Condition

Depression is not the only problem that can be caused by some larger problem in the body. There are many medical conditions that can cause mental disorders. These include brain injuries, diseases of the nervous system, breathing problems, tumors, especially in the brain, cancer, nutritional or **metabolic** problems, digestive diseases, skin diseases, **lupus**, and other autoimmune diseases.

The brain uses chemicals, called neurotransmitters, to send messages back and forth across synapses. Depression and other mood disorders can result from problems with neurotransmitters related to how they are released, how much is released, and how much is taken back by the cell sending the neurotransmitters.

A category of medications, called antidepressants, can help people with these problems. Antidepressants work by adjusting the neurotransmitters. These adjustments affect how people think, act, and feel. For some psychological disorders, psychiatric drugs seem like a miracle cure. For others, they can only control symptoms. Most of the time, therapy is tried before medication, and drug treatment typically is used together with **psychotherapy**.

Neuroscientists estimate that there are about 100 billion neurons in the human brain. Each neuron may be connected to up to 10,000 other neurons.

Therapy

For many people with depression, medicine is not enough to solve the problem. Most people benefit from some form of therapy in addition to the antidepressant. People often call psychotherapy counseling or talk therapy. It is a form of help that involves talking with someone, such as a psychiatrist, psychologist, nurse, social worker, or counselor. There are various types of therapy.

COGNITIVE THERAPY. Cognitive therapy focuses on helping someone with a mood disorder learn how to think differently. Patients learn to replace negative thoughts with positive ones. People with depression often tell themselves, "I never do anything right." Cognitive therapy helps them try to replace those thoughts with more positive ones, such as, "I tried my best." This may sound like a small change, but, over time, new habits of thought can help relieve depression.

IF THE DOCTOR PRESCRIBES MEDICATION

The American Academy of Child and Adolescent Psychiatry recommends asking a doctor questions about any medication that has been prescribed.

1. What is the medication's name? What are its other names?

2. Has this medication helped other people my age? How?

3. What will the medication do for me? How long will it take to work?

4. What side effects can I expect? How long will they last? Will they go away in time?

5. What other rare and dangerous side effects are possible?

6. Can I become addicted to this medication? Can it be abused?

7. What will be my dosage to start? What is the recommended dosage?

8. Will I have to take special tests to monitor this drug in my system, such as blood tests, heart tests, liver tests, and so on?

9. What foods or medicines should I avoid while taking this drug?

10. Are there any activities I cannot do while I am on this drug?

11. How long will I have to be on this medication?

12. How do I go off this medication safely?

13. What do I do if I have problems with this drug?

14. Should I tell my school officials or school nurse that I am taking this drug?

15. Who else needs to know that I am on this drug?

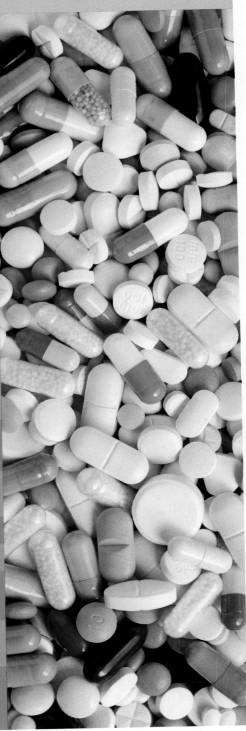

BEHAVIORAL THERAPY. This form of therapy focuses on helping people change the way they act. It equips the person to behave in ways that will make him or her feel more fulfilled and satisfied. Behavioral therapy also helps people unlearn old patterns or habits that only make them feel worse. It is quite common for someone to undergo cognitive-behavioral therapy, which addresses both how people think and what they do.

A doctor can help patients decide what kind of therapy will work best for them and where to find it.

INTERPERSONAL THERAPY. This type of therapy helps people improve relationship and communication skills, resolve conflict, and deal with unresolved feelings of anger or grief. The focus is primarily on how to get along with others in healthy ways.

PSYCHODYNAMIC THERAPY. Psychodynamic therapy examines past experiences to try to understand how the patient thinks, feels, and acts in the present. The therapist will tend to focus less on "how to" skills and more on thoughts and feelings. This type of therapy usually lasts longer than other forms of treatment.

SUPPORTIVE THERAPY. In most types of therapy, doctors and therapists stay objective. They do not take a side or tell the patient what to do. In supportive therapy, the therapist acts more as a coach, encouraging the patient to find new habits of thought and action.

Take a Deeper Look

Find out more about the different types of therapy available for treating depression. What are the pros and cons of the different types? Record your answers in a table, with pros on one side and cons on the other.

Managing Depression

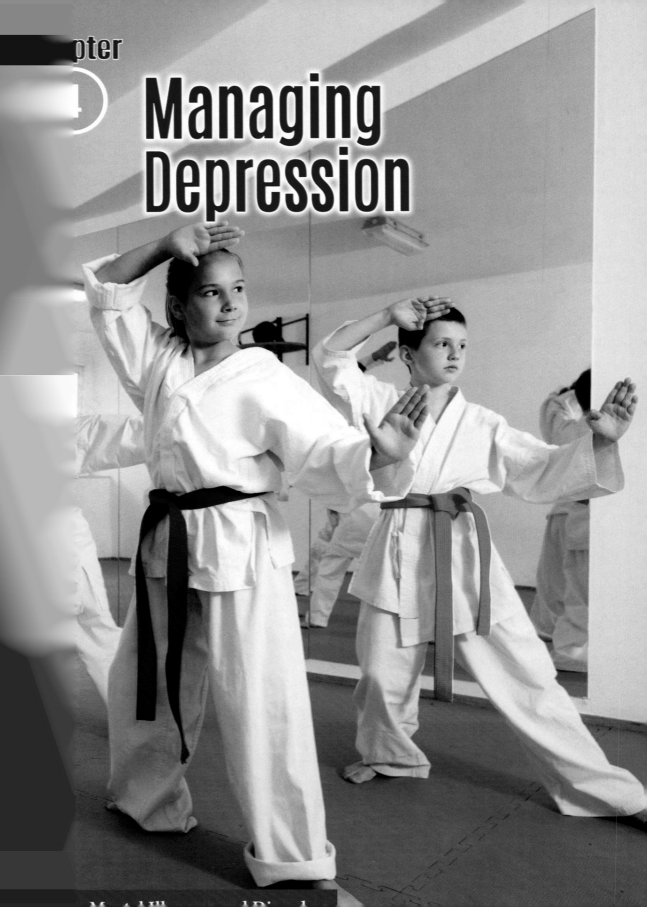

There apy and medication are two important ways of handling mood disorders. However, there are a lot of other things people can do to help depression.

Exercise

In a study done at Duke University, in North Carolina, 156 adults with major depression were given one of three treatment options.

1. Exercise for 45 minutes three times a week, but do not take medication.
2. Take medication, but do not exercise.
3. Do both. Exercise for 45 minutes three times a week and take medication.

After four months, the people who only exercised improved about as much as the people who only took medication or who did both. After an additional six months, the people who continued to exercise regularly were the least likely to have their depression come back again. Exercise can improve self-esteem and provides a number of health benefits.

Exercise can lead to increased energy, better sleep, and a healthier heart and lungs.

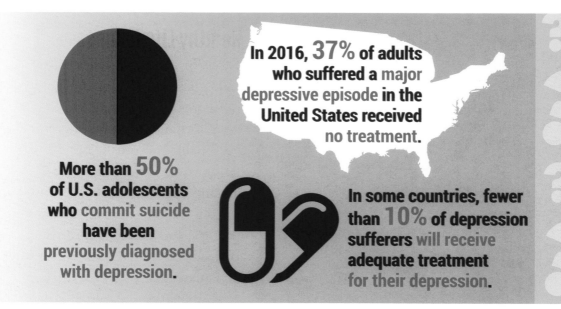

In 2016, 37% of adults who suffered a major depressive episode in the United States received no treatment.

More than 50% of U.S. adolescents who commit suicide have been previously diagnosed with depression.

In some countries, fewer than 10% of depression sufferers will receive adequate treatment for their depression.

Alternative Medicine and Depression

Homeopathy is a form of alternative medicine that treats disease and disorders from a very different perspective than traditional medicine. It looks at a person's entire physical and mental being, rather than dividing a patient into various symptoms and disorders. Homeopathic medicine uses tiny doses to stimulate the body's ability to heal itself. In some cases, these doses may be administered only once every few months or years. Some people believe that homeopathy offers safe, natural alternatives that can supplement or replace conventional pharmaceutical treatments. However, homeopathic remedies are not **regulated**, which means there is no guarantee that they are absolutely safe. That is why it is important never to take any supplements without talking it over with a doctor or another trusted adult.

Exercise can be a great antidote to the low energy, sleep problems, low self-esteem, and increased anger that mood disorders can cause. It is important to talk to the doctor before starting an exercise program, however. If he or she agrees, start slowly. Pick an exercise you enjoy. Any exercise you want to do is better than something you do not truly like. Aim for 30 minutes of **continuous** exercise at least four days a week.

Lack of sleep or disrupted sleep increases tension and irritability, which are often associated with mood disorders.

Healthy Life Choices

SLEEP. Sleeping too little or too much is a common symptom of depression. Making some simple changes can help, such as establishing a routine of always going to bed and getting up at around the same time, avoiding naps during the day, keeping televisions, phones, and tablets out of the bedroom, and avoiding soda, coffee, chocolate, and other foods that contain the stimulant caffeine.

NUTRITION. It is common for people with depression to crave so-called comfort foods, which are often high in sugar or salt. These foods tend to lack other types of nutrition. That is why people refer to them as having empty calories. Eating too much of these foods can actually make a person feel worse. On the other hand, eating fruits, vegetables, and whole grains every day will create a feeling of fullness in the short term, and they may help a person's mood in the long term.

Several studies have suggested that eating a healthy diet is associated with a decreased risk of depression.

AVOID DRUGS AND ALCOHOL. It is true that alcohol and drugs such as marijuana can change mood. People with depression may be very tempted to use these chemicals to make themselves feel better for a short time. Unfortunately, these effects wear off and leave them feeling worse than when they started. They can also have a very negative effect on physical health and on the ability to sleep.

Take a Deeper Look

Some people with depression find that keeping a journal can be very helpful. Try keeping your own journal for at least a week. Every day, write down a sentence or two that describes your mood or moods. Also write a short list of events that happened and how you felt about them. Finally, keep track of how much you slept, how much you exercised, and what you ate. Do you notice any connections between these physical activities and your changing moods?

Reach Out

People who feel depressed are often **listless**. They do not feel like they have the energy for their friends anymore. Nearly every activity feels like it is just too much work. The truth is, taking part in regular activities can be important for recovery. Friends, hobbies, and physical activity can all help take people out of themselves and forget their problems for a while. While that is easy to say, of course, it can be very difficult to do.

Depression can make it feel like the simplest activities are totally impossible. Getting dressed for school is like climbing a huge mountain. The thought of calling a friend can seem impossible. It is important to remember that the voice saying "I can't do it" is the depression, not the person. Staying connected to friends and family is one of the most important things people with depression can do. Even taking care of a pet can help someone feel better.

Looking to the Future

How people treat depression is a deeply personal choice. It should involve the person, his or her family, and a mental health professional. With so many options available today, most people should be able to find a strategy that works for them.

With love and support, along with the proper medical treatment, people with depression can get better. When people are willing to take the risk of asking for help, they can go on to lead happy, fulfilled lives.

Letting close friends and loved ones help can be an important step in any treatment of depression.

Living with Depression

The challenges of living with depression are not easy to deal with. However, with time, patience, and understanding, it is possible to help a friend or loved one who has the illness.

Ask Questions

Rather than saying, "I know how you feel," ask how the person feels. Let the person know he can talk to you without being judged.

Be a Good Listener

Often, people with depression just want someone to listen carefully. Be prepared to listen rather than give advice.

Keep the Invitations Coming

A depressed friend might turn you down a lot. Do not stop asking. If nothing else, it will help her to know you still want her around.

Support the Treatment

If the person is seeing a therapist or taking medication, or both, encourage him or her to keep the treatment going.

Take Suicidal Thoughts Seriously

If a friend mentions suicidal thoughts, be sure to let an adult know. Do not keep it to yourself. Your friend needs help.

Accept Setbacks

It is difficult to move out of depression. Support your friend or family member even though they may be finding things hard.

Depression over Time

Mood disorders have been around for as long as people have. It is only recently, though, with advances in technology and knowledge of the human brain, that doctors have begun to understand the causes of depression and how to treat them effectively.

C. 400 BC

Greek physician Hippocrates describes melancholia as being "fear and despondencies if they last a long time." He believes it is caused by an excess of black **bile** in the human system. Melancholy is an important concept for 2,500 years after Hippocrates.

1899 AD

German psychiatrist Emil Kraepelin publishes the sixth edition of his *Psychiatric Teaching Manual*. He uses the term "depression" rather than "melancholy." The term "melancholy" passes out of general medical use, although it is still used by some therapists.

1912

Austrian doctor Sigmund Freud compares melancholia to mourning in his 1917 paper "Mourning and Melancholia." He describes how the sufferer believes in his or her own blame, inferiority, and unworthiness.

Many people feel ashamed about having a mental disorder such as depression. However, having a problem with brain chemistry is no more shameful than having a broken limb.

1960

The first **benzodiazepine** drug is marketed as Librium and is recognized to be effective in treating the immediate symptoms of depression. By the mid-1970s, benzodiazepines become the most prescribed drugs in the world.

1980

The third edition of the *Diagnostic and Statistical Manual of Mental Disorders* (*DSM-III*) lists a pattern of symptoms for major depressive disorder. A variety of forms of depression, from persistent depressive disorder to psychotic episodes, are now recognized.

2017

A research team at Columbia University Medical Center, New York, found that the drug ketamine, an anesthetic and pain killer, worked significantly better at stopping suicidal thoughts in depressed patients than a commonly used sedative.

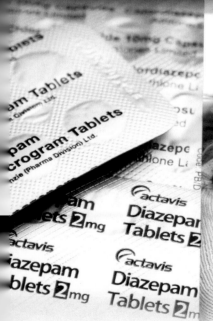

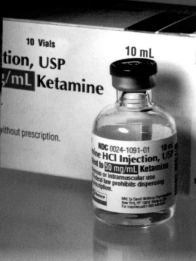

Quiz

1 What does the word "depression" literally mean?

2 What are the two main types of depression?

3 What amount of exercise has been found to help relieve depression?

4 What does "SAD" stand for?

5 What percentage of Americans struggle with depression every year?

6 What gland in the body can cause depression?

7 Who can be affected by postpartum depression?

8 What branch of medicine do pediatricians specialize in?

9 What is a synapse?

10 How do antidepressants work?

ANSWERS

1 "Pushing down" **2** Major depressive disorder and persistent depressive disorder **3** 30 minutes 4 times a week **4** Seasonal affective disorder **5** 26 percent **6** The thyroid gland **7** Mothers who have recently given birth **8** Treating children and young adults **9** The gap between two neurons **10** They adjust neurotransmitters in the brain.

[30]   Mental Illnesses and Disorders

Key Words

benzodiazepine: a type of drug used as a tranquillizer

bile: a liquid made by the liver that helps digestion

chronic: a problem that is ongoing and does not get better over time

continuous: ongoing, not stopping and starting

criteria: a group of standards

homeopathy: the treatment of disease with naturally occurring substances

listless: without energy or enthusiasm

lupus: any of various diseases characterized by skin inflammation

menstruation: the monthly shedding of blood by women

metabolic: the process by which energy is created in the body

objective: not based on personal feelings but on direct observation

pediatrician: a doctor who treats children and young adults

postpartum: after giving birth

psychosis: a severe mental disorder where the person loses touch with reality

psychotherapy: a treatment for mental disorders

regulated: something that is overseen by an authority, such as the government

severity: how intense or serious something is

strategies: plans for solving problems

subjective: based on personal feelings and experiences

thyroid: a gland at the base of the neck that releases hormones

trigger: something that causes something else to happen

Index

advice about depression   23, 24, 25, 26, 27
alcohol and drugs   14, 25
antidepressants   12, 19, 30

behavioral therapy   21
bipolar disorder   7, 13
brain chemistry   9, 19, 29

causes of depression   9, 11, 12, 13, 14, 15
cognitive therapy   19

Diagnostic and Statistical Manual of Mental Disorders (DSM)   13, 29
diet and nutrition   25
disruptive mood dysregulation disorder (DMDD)   13
doctor, talking to   17, 18, 24

exercise   12, 23, 24, 30

food   8, 24, 25
friends   5, 6, 8, 26

homeopathy   24

interpersonal therapy   21

light therapy   12

major depressive disorder   6, 7, 8
major depressive episode (MDE)   7, 8, 9
medical conditions and depression   13, 14, 18
medication   12, 15, 18, 19, 20, 23, 27
mood disorder   7, 19, 23, 24, 28

neurotransmitters   19, 30
number of people with depression   5, 11, 17

persistent depressive disorder   8, 9, 17, 29
pets   26
physical disabilities   13, 14
postpartum depression   15
premenstrual dysphoric disorder (PMDD)   14, 15
premenstrual syndrome (PMS)   14, 15
psychodynamic therapy   21
psychotherapy   19

seasonal affective disorder (SAD)   11, 12, 15, 30
sleep   7, 8, 12, 18, 23, 24, 25
supportive therapy   21
symptoms of depression   5, 6, 7, 8, 12, 14, 17, 29

therapy   15, 18, 19, 21, 23

weight   7, 8, 12

Log on to www.av2books.com

AV² by Weigl brings you media enhanced books that support active learning. Go to www.av2books.com, and enter the special code found on page 2 of this book. You will gain access to enriched and enhanced content that supplements and complements this book. Content includes video, audio, weblinks, quizzes, a slide show, and activities.

AV² Online Navigation

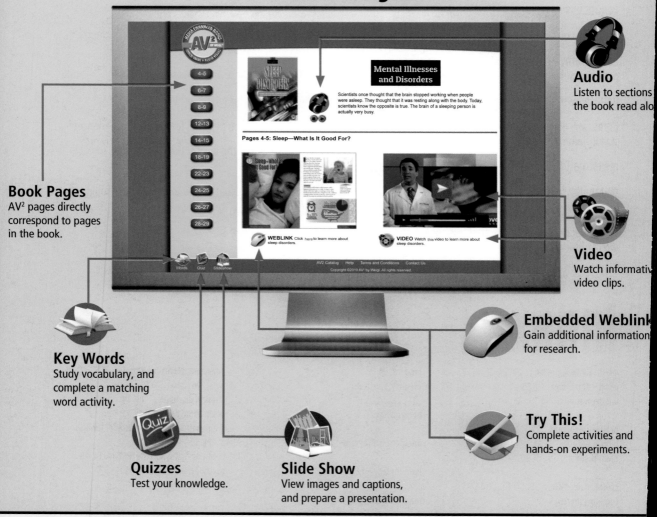

Audio
Listen to sections
the book read alo

Book Pages
AV² pages directly correspond to pages in the book.

Video
Watch informativ
video clips.

Key Words
Study vocabulary, and complete a matching word activity.

Embedded Weblink
Gain additional information
for research.

Try This!
Complete activities and hands-on experiments.

Quizzes
Test your knowledge.

Slide Show
View images and captions, and prepare a presentation.

AV² was built to bridge the gap between print and digital. We encourage you to tell us what you like and what you want to see in the future.

Sign up to be an AV² Ambassador at www.av2books.com/ambassador.

Due to the dynamic nature of the Internet, some of the URLs and activities provided as part of AV² by Weigl may have changed or ceased to exist. AV² by Weigl accepts no responsibility for any such changes. All media enhanced books are regularly monitored to update addresses and sites in a timely manner. Contact AV² by Weigl at 1-866-649-3445 or av2books@weigl.com with any questions, comments, or feedback.